THE *art* OF RELATING

a primer for love

by

Christine Kniffen, LCSW

ACKNOWLEDGEMENTS

This book is dedicated to the school of hard knocks, where I learned much about the ways of love. Equally, this endeavor could not be possible without the experience and knowledge gained from deciphering the patterns and perspectives of my numerous, terrific clients throughout the years. I hope this book serves as the basis for many great conversations between couples, friends and those just embarking in the realm of love. I have found my true love and you can too. I can't express enough my gratitude for the invaluable editing assistance from my dear friend Nancy Brier. Also, I would like to send a very special thanks to Jessica Kinnard for endless work she did on the cover design, press kit and quite frankly putting it all together for print. Lastly, I dedicate this book to my grandmother who lived to the wonderful age of 103 years. She is deeply missed.

TABLE OF CONTENTS

SECTION 1

WHAT WE DO

The Art of Relating: A Primer For Love
© 2012 By Christine Kniffen
www.christinekniffen.com • www.theartofrelatingbook.com
ISBN #: 978-0-61-548258-3

The Art of Relating

CHAPTER 1

STOP CHOOSING
EMOTIONALLY UNAVAILABLE

Lying in the fetal position, while sobbing to the depths of my soul, I could not understand why no one wanted to love me. Why was I always left? What was I doing wrong and what was so wrong with me? This feeling was not so much in direct correlation to the relationship that had just ended, but rather the powerful, cumulative effect of the same scenario and subsequent feelings felt at the ending of all my previous relationships. This is what I learned…..

It's one of the most common complaints I hear from the individuals who come to my office for Relationship Coaching sessions. "Why do I keep finding people who are emotionally unavailable every time I try to have a relationship?" I hear the resounding chorus, "I don't know that they are unavailable when I first start seeing them." "So how am I supposed to keep this from happening?" Have you ever heard the saying, "unavailable picks unavailable?" Well, at some point the concept of choosing "unavailable" in relationships is something many of us need to pause and consider if we are to move forward and stop the pattern from continuing. I realize that this observation sparks an immediate defensive reaction for many of us. I continually picked the emotionally unavailable in my earlier years, and when someone mentioned it to me I thought they were crazy. "How am I emotionally unavailable?" I spat back. Well, I reluctantly came to understand that I too had work to do in this area if I was to stop this unfulfilling pattern and finally find a relationship that worked. Emotional unavailability equates to an inability to be fully emotionally vulnerable with another. In trying to make progress in this area, it is important first to understand precisely what it means to be emotionally vulnerable, identify the two levels of vulnerability and finally begin to take an honest assessment of our own capabilities in this area. After all, it is unfair to expect something more from another than you are able to do yourself.

So, what does it mean to be emotionally vulnerable? Vulnerability equates to risk. In order to be emotionally vulnerable, you have to be willing to face the fears of risk. Vulnerability has two levels. Level one starts when you first meet someone for dating. Level one involves telling the other person those things about you that make you feel uncomfortable or embarrassed. It's risky because your history may include experiences that you think may cause the other person to run for the hills once they find out. You know the scenario- your friend says did you tell him that your mother is crazy, that your brother is in jail, that you declared bankruptcy last year or that you tend to struggle with insecurity? Most people find that they do a pretty decent job of being vulnerable on the level one type of issues.

However, learning to be vulnerable on the second level is much harder as it involves greater emotional risk. It involves tearing down those protective walls and really letting another into your most intimate fears, anxieties, self-doubt and deepest desires.

The second level of vulnerability involves being able to sit across from your partner and be fully honest with him or her as to how you are feeling. It requires an ability to calmly, without blame or anger, let them know how something they do affects you and either hurts your feelings or makes you afraid. After all, hurt and fear are the real feelings that always drive pissed off or mad. It is risky to tell your partner that they repeatedly hurt your feelings when you go out to gatherings together, because he or she talks to everyone but you for the majority of the evening. And, when they start talking to other people they never seem to include you in the conversation, despite you standing right there. It's hard to say that it makes you feel insignificant in their life and that you don't feel special and important to them in the same way that you work to show them just the opposite. Getting down to this level is scary and risky because they could say that you are just overly sensitive or insecure that you seem to need that much attention. Or, they could laugh at you and tell you that your feelings are childish. Instead, we often resort to the less scary tactic of ridiculing someone for having virtually ignored us much of the evening. We show them anger and expect them to understand and validate our feelings. However, if we get mad it doesn't usually end the argument because our partner then gets defensive and the message is not received. Once you understand these two levels of vulnerability, it is time to do some honest self-assessment.

After I provide this framework for the concept of vulnerability to clients who complain they gravitate to the emotionally unavailable, I then ask them for an honest assessment of their abilities to be vulnerable at both of these levels. When I do I routinely hear a softly muttered, "I don't do very well at the second level" or "I don't do level two at all." "Well," I say, "is it really fair to expect something from another person that you can't do either?" That moment is when the figurative light bulb goes off for most clients and they then make this important connection. It isn't really about "picking" unavailable. Instead, it is about staying too long and putting up with the emotionally unavailable longer than you should. If you could be more vulnerable and face the fear of having to leave if the right ingredients are not present for the relationship to work, then you would do the leaving early on and not have to endure a pattern of getting in relationships with emotionally unavailable people. Believe me when I say that the ability to be emotionally vulnerable with another by honestly stating your feelings and stating your needs is a work in progress for most of us. It is scary to be vulnerable because we may be laughed at or simply dismissed, which both work to leave us feeling that you don't care. If we find we continually get a negative response when we try to be vulnerable with our feelings, we our then forced to come face-to-face with the real possibility that we may in fact be in a relationship where the other person is unwilling or unable to join us on the second level of vulnerability. Without achieving both levels of vulnerability in or relationship we will never really have the emotional intimacy, hence level of connectedness that we all yearn to feel.

The secret to stopping the pattern of hooking up with someone who is emotionally unavailable starts with you. Ask yourself if you are truly proficient at being vulnerable at both levels. You will never feel validated in your feelings nor will you get your needs met if you don't master the two levels of vulnerability yourself. Tear down those walls and learn to be vulnerable. If you do, you will finally insist upon the relationship that you deserve.

CHAPTER 2

UNREALISTIC EXPECTATIONS

Unrealistic expectations were perhaps one of my biggest impediments to being happy in a relationship for many years. For so long I had envisioned a kind of idyllic oneness that simply did not exist. I in essence placed a huge burden on you to fulfill great emotional expectations I had, when I could neither identify them nor fulfill them myself. Add in the fact that I continually gravitated to people who were also emotionally unavailable and you can see how my relationships were really quite doomed from the start. This is what I learned.....

Disappointment and disillusionment in relationships almost invariably stems from unmet and perhaps unrealistic expectations of what a relationship should look like. Unrealistic expectations are responsible for much of the hardships that couples experience. These relationship expectations are influenced in large part by the types of relationships our parents had, by the myths perpetuated by the media and popular culture and by our own desires resulting from an underdeveloped sense of self. All of these factors shape our thoughts and perceptions of what a relationship should look like.

First, let's start with the types of expectations that result from our parent's relationship. The relationship modeled by our parents is perhaps the greatest influence on our expectations of what a relationship should look like. People tend to go one of two ways with what they saw growing up. For example, if someone grows up in a home where parents fight and argue much of the time, they will most likely either emulate this behavior or vow never to fight with their partner. This particular experience sets the stage for relationship difficulties in two different ways. If you emulate this behavior with someone who did not grow up with fighting and arguing, this heightened discord will be entirely too unfamiliar and unacceptable for your partner to tolerate. Your expectation that this behavior is okay is unrealistic. On the other hand, if you vowed never to argue and let every disagreement slide for the sake of peace, you will run into a whole other set of problems. If you find yourself stuffing your feelings in order to keep peace, you will ultimately feel unheard and invalidated in regard to your feelings. Eventually, these built up repressed feelings will lead to total resentment. Your expectation that someone should be a mind reader is unrealistic as well. Remember, perception is everything.

Second, popular culture has done a great disservice in its perpetuation of unrealistic expectations with regards to love and relationships. Television, movies and books all work to model unachievable states in love and relationships. The concept of love at first sight, the idea of virtually knowing each other's thoughts and the idea of unending romance are just a few of the myths enhanced by popular culture. Images of unrealistic love barrage our psyches. We may know intellectually that these myths are not true. However, our emotional side still holds out for the images that have been fed to us through the media, advertising and countless movies. This disparity between our intellectual side and our emotional side causes much of the disillusionment and unhappiness we experience in relationships.

Lastly, our levels of self-esteem greatly affect our expectations of a relationship and what we think it should provide us. It all starts in childhood. Families that do not function optimally can be characterized by such traits as the inability to communicate effectively, to compromise and problem-solve, to identify and ask that needs be met, to demonstrate affection and to tolerate and encourage free thought from their children. These much needed life skills should ideally be taught and modeled by the family. However, if they are not properly modeled, children may be left with an underdeveloped sense of self. They lack the confidence and skills needed to make decisions, trust their instincts, validate themselves and generally feel worthy of love in many cases. This under developed sense of self in turn can foster the formation of unrealistic expectations from others including excessive needs for validation, confidence building, reassurance, unconditional loyalty, etc. These needs are unrealistic in that no one but yourself can fill these needs for you. This places entirely too much pressure on the partner in the relationship to do for you what you cannot do for yourself. Decreased levels of self-esteem are fairly common by-products experienced by children who come from dysfunctional families. As long as we look to someone else to fill these needs for ourselves, we will be disappointed and disillusioned time and time again in our relationships.

Take some time to assess your relationship expectations. Are they realistic or are they off skew? Do you have a pattern of setting yourself up for continual disappointment? Many people find that they are highly influenced by the type of relationship modeled by their parents. Then they work to change these expectations, view relationships differently and date with a new perspective. If you take this step you just may be able to experience something different in your next or current relationship.

CHAPTER 3

THE BLAME GAME

As much as I would love to report otherwise, I have to admit that I was a rather adept participant in the blame game. I am very sensitive and seem to get my feelings hurt quite easily. I almost always felt right about my side of the argument. Therefore, the only thing left for you to be was wrong. I felt perfectly justified in this accuracy, not trying to be a jerk, but simply feeling it to be correct. I seemed to think that the level of intensity of my feelings as to being right, somehow correlated with supposed accuracy of this premise which further supported my justification. However, I now realize that this simply isn't so. This is what I learned......

Have you ever been in a relationship where the blame game seems to permeate everything?

It is something that I see operating in full force with many of the individuals who come into my office for marriage and couples counseling. Each one is blaming the other for their unhappiness and each one feels that they are definitely on the side of right. It's not as if anyone is making this up. Rather, each person feels strongly that they are right and the other person is wrong. However, since each person feels they are in the right, a great power struggle ensues and the relationship has grounded to a complete halt with no real potential for growth. And, as a wise therapist told me years ago, if a relationship can't grow, then it can't last. The blame game is very detrimental to both your relationships and your personal growth as well. It creates a great power struggle in the relationship, it prevents you from perfecting one of the most fundamental relationship skills known as compromise and it stunts your own growth as blaming another allows you to shirk personal responsibility and accountability for your own happiness.

I like to refer to The Great Standoff when working with couples. I am speaking of the classic power struggle that can happen in a relationship. Since neither person is doing a good job of validating their partner's feelings, each one is holding on tighter to their position and sense of righteousness to the point of complete paralysis in the relationship. They even go so far as to blame each other for their particular behaviors. When I try to call anyone on a non-productive behavior, in terms of relating or communicating, they attempt to justify its acceptability by becoming defensive and declaring that the other person does it too. Therein lies the loop and the endless circular motion of the blame game. In this paralyzed loop, relationship growth is not possible. Worse yet, the wounding begins and can become almost insurmountable if left unattended for too long of a stretch. This wounding allows for people who once loved each other get to the point that they can't stand each other. These couples suffer because they have never learned the fundamental relationship skill known as compromise.

It is not possible to have a healthy, fulfilling relationship without its presence. Again and again, people struggle with this concept as it pertains to relationships. "I'm not going to compromise who I am," becomes an emotionally charged, declarative statement from individuals who have put up with bad behavior from partners in past relationships. So, now we are going to have a power struggle over compromise. If you are not dating yourself, you will need to learn to compromise in a relationship. No, you don't have to compromise on things that are adamantly opposed to your personal value system. You can't be in a relationship with someone who chronically lies if you are about truth and honesty. But, if you make your feelings on the matter known and nothing changes, then it is you who needs to walk. Don't spend years blaming this other person for your unhappiness over his or her lying. This example shows exactly how people use the blame game, often unwittingly, to avoid taking personal responsibility and accountability for their own happiness and ultimate destiny as a whole.

If you get into a habit of participating in the blame game in your relationships, you are stunting your personal growth as well as that of the relationship. Blaming someone else abdicates you of personal responsibility for creating the life that you say you want. You have heard the old cliché that says "the only thing that gets in your way is you." If you find your relationship stuck in the blame game, you may require professional help to stop the cycle. If your partner will not participate, you may just have to move on, as the relationship cannot grow and neither can you. Stop blaming others for not having the life you want. Take the necessary steps to become more self-aware. Therapy is designed to help with just that issue. One of the main things therapy does is to help people reach their own potential. Self-awareness, through insight and reflection, is the only path to achieving that goal. It starts with stopping the blame game and stopping the patterns that are keeping you stuck. Great things in life don't just drop down from the sky. You have to go out and make them happen. Stopping the blame game is the first step to getting you started down the right path to manifest your ultimate destiny.

CHAPTER 4

STABILITY VERSUS EXCITEMENT

I think early on I was sort of addicted to the excitement that happens in the beginning of a relationship. Not the type of excitement that is healthy, but rather the sort of up and down emotional drama that always accompanies an unavailable partner. By drama I really refer to the miserable, emotional roller coaster of feelings that I suffered. These no doubt manifested themselves through a combination of my insecurity and their inconsistency in ability to be present in the relationship, along with the obvious ambiguity in their degree of commitment. This dynamic always kept me off guard. It certainly took the focus off of me and as with any good addiction, it allowed me to check temporarily out of my life. As a result of this up and down nature, the relationship's foundation was never stable and therefore had nothing tangible to build upon. This is what I learned….

What are you really looking for in a relationship? What do most people really want from a healthy partnership? Stability is what most people want whether they know it or not. Many things in life are unpredictable. Therefore, it is essential that we create some sense of stability somewhere in our lives. This is exactly what we need from a relationship. Sure, there are no guarantees that it will last, but you don't need to be in a relationship that constantly adds to the world's unpredictability.

Have you heard your friends say, "he is nice, polite, has a good job, seems stable...but I'm just not attracted to him because he's not very exciting?" If you need exciting, then why don't you take up bungee jumping? This is your life, and you need to create your own excitement. It is not the responsibility of your partner to entertain you because you do not know how to do it yourself. This type of pressure often drives a relationship apart. If you are not comfortable in your own skin and do know how to rejuvenate yourself with things that bring you peace, joy and excitement, you will never be satisfied in any relationship. Until you solve these issues for yourself you will always have unrealistic expectations that put unnecessary pressure on the relationship to give you what you cannot give yourself. In a stable relationship you have plenty of energy to work on you. In a roller coaster relationship, your emotions are on overload and there is nothing left in the reserve tank.

Many people in long-term relationships will describe themselves as good companions. However, they too were not entirely comfortable with that word in the beginning. Have you ever met the couple that almost sounds apologetic for having a stable relationship? They will often say things such as, "I guess we are pretty boring, we like to stay at home a have good friends over for dinner." However, as time passes they become grateful for this "boring stability" when they continue to hear horror stories from their friends cycling in and out of bad relationships.

Most people are looking for companionship on some level. We all want a best friend to talk with and someone to snuggle up to when we wake up in the morning. This stable companionship is at the core of most good, solid relationships. A relationship with a stable foundation can weather many of the storms that life throws us. If you need excitement, create it for yourself. Be thankful if you have "boring stability" in your relationship. After all, you may just still have it this time next year.

CHAPTER 5

SEPARATING "I" AND "WE"

Learning how to be an independent person, while functioning in a relationship had always been extremely hard for me to do. I yearned for continued togetherness in my early relationships. It was as if this dynamic provided a calming effect for my own insecurities. When we were apart for any given length of time, my mind would begin to torture me with thoughts of problems and possible finality to a union I so thought I needed. It wasn't until several years into my relationship that I understood why constant togetherness was not good. This is what I learned…..

Separating "I" and "we" is perhaps one of the hardest relationship skills that must be developed and continuously fine-tuned. Enmeshment is a term used in family therapy to describe unclear or permeable boundaries between particular family members in a family system. Simply speaking, enmeshment refers to a lack of separation between "I" and "We." It is not uncommon for individuals to lose their sense of identity while in a relationship. It has happened to some degree to all of us. We find ourselves becoming like the other person and doing many of the things that they like to do. Think back to the end of a particular relationship that you have had. Do you remember that feeling of not knowing how to fill your space and time? Do you remember that empty slate feeling in which you had to find yourself again? Do you remember wondering who you were and what you liked to do prior to that relationship starting? It is not hard to empathize with the depths of loneliness that many of us have felt when having to go through that type of situation. A balanced life is the key to happiness. Likewise, a balanced relationship is optimal and must be reached in order to achieve longevity and provide a good sense of security. A relationship can be out of balance by either not enough separation between the individuals or too much separation between partners.

Relationships with a lack of healthy separation usually have some predictable patterns. Often, one of the partners is living their life and the other is simply going along with things, as being together becomes the main priority over meeting their own personal needs. This is not a totally conscious decision. Rather, it is a pattern that gets developed at the beginning of the relationship often through one partner focusing too much on the other. However, this pattern is hurtful to both partners. The partner who always goes along just to be near almost invariably ends up resentful after years of personal neglect. This junction is the point at which the other partner learns that you never liked or enjoyed certain things that the two of you did together. This partner is now suddenly hurt and baffled to realize this when he or she had no idea. Many couples have to work very hard to make a smooth transition from the blissful beginning stage to that of two separate adults each with their own lives. A lack of separation between "I" and "we" is driven, in part, by fear. This includes the fear of never finding anyone, as well as the fear of having it go away once we have found it. Conversely, there can be too much separation between two people.

Too much separation can take place on either the physical level or on an emotional level. Someone who schedules most of their evenings with commitments to various organizations, meetings or sporting leagues really doesn't have the time to date you. Therefore, be honest with yourself and your needs. How much time do you need with someone in order to feel satisfied? Determine your answer prior to beginning dating. Also, as a general rule of thumb, the "out-of-town" relationship usually does not work (I did say usually). Equally important, is the need for emotional closeness. It is necessary for a relationship to develop intimacy through good levels of communication. Nothing can make you feel lonelier than living with someone who does not open up and share his or her feelings. The presence of a closed, emotional wall will result in too much separation and is not the optimal arena for true intimacy to develop either.

Think hard on the idea of separation. Do you have a healthy balance between "I" and "We" in your current relationship? Talk with your partner about this concept and decide what changes can be implemented to better balance things for the two of you. If you are just starting to date, keep this in mind as your relationship patterns begin to develop so you won't have so much work to do later.

CHAPTER 6

LOVE AND FEAR

It wasn't until many years later, and having by then found a great relationship, that I realized I had been expending a lot of mental energy trying to keep from getting hurt in all my previous relationships. I analyzed every nuance, almost looking for something wrong so as to avoid being blind-sided and getting hurt. I clearly tuned out rather obvious red flags, so as not to have to face the fact that the relationship would not work and therefore, again, not be hurt when it ended. The reality is that we cannot protect ourselves from emotional hurt. And, the sooner we accept and embrace this fact, the faster the fear lessens its grip and its control in our quest for love. This is what I learned…..

Have you been deeply hurt? Were you previously convinced that you had found "the one" only to see it crumble right before your eyes? Have you ever told yourself that you won't let "that" happen again? If you can relate to any of these statements, then perhaps you have felt burned by love. A lot of people go around as the walking wounded when it comes to love. As a result, individuals are often afraid on some level to try again. Their heads may be willing, but their hearts are walled up to some degree and need to be set free. If you find yourself in this position, it's time to consider a few important concepts. Many of us need to learn how to return to a lighthearted sense of fun regarding relationships, how to stop being afraid of the possible fall and how to fight those old tapes that tell us we will never find anyone.

Really good relationships tend to have a healthy atmosphere of ease and play. When you are interested in someone and begin dating, you should think of it merely as an exercise in getting to know someone.

Don't make it any more than it is. You need time to see how you hang together, laugh together and just be together. Keep it light. Life is serious enough and you sure don't want to live within the confines of a heavy relationship that is too serious all of the time. On the first date I often advise clients to pay attention to three factors. Is there laughter and spontaneity? Does the conversation flow freely? This is much more important than whether or not you know with absolute certainty that this is someone capable of giving you a long-term relationship. The need for this guarantee, driven by a fear of getting hurt again, results in us going about it backwards. First, decide if there is a nice flow of energy and an ease of compatibility. If there is then take a deep breath and have a few more dates. It's really not in your control, as relationships require two. Put it out to the universe and if it's meant to be, it will happen.

A second concept to think about is our fear of the fall. Each relationship we have had in the past prepares us for greater and greater heights in love and intimacy. Often the last relationship we were in had been the most to date in terms of getting what we thought we wanted. Therefore, we clung tightly to it because who wanted to let go of the closest they had come to the very thing they so desired? Last time we fell off the ladder, it hurt. Therefore, people are understandably afraid to go to higher levels of intimacy with someone because the next fall might really be bad. After having experienced this fall, you have arrived at a pivotal point in your journey to love. It is at this crucial junction that you must decide what the real goal is. Is it to search out guaranteed endurance in a relationship, or is the goal really to experience climbing to the top of the mountain with someone? Some individuals strive for higher and higher levels of experience, while some people want safety and comfort to the point of settling. Neither view is necessarily right or wrong. However, it might be a good idea to contemplate this concept and decide which goal really works best for you. I personally think that experiencing higher and deeper levels is much more exciting.

Lastly, if you have decided that you want to head to the top of the mountain, you have to let go of any old tapes telling you that you will never find anyone. This fear actually gets in the way of climbing to the top because you are more concerned with finding that perfect relationship, as opposed to being open to experiencing the greater heights. Negative messages regarding love work to either keep us stuck in the past or obsessed with protecting ourselves in the future. The result is that we don't live in the here and now and we miss out on the fun and the play with the person we have just met. Many people come to understand with age, but it seems somehow elusive from our concepts when we are younger and more naïve. Love is all around us. There is no shortage. We just need to learn to open our eyes and experience it in its purist form, without all of the tired distortions we put on it due to our fears based on previous painful experiences.

In short, turn off those nagging, negative messages and relax. Begin your approach to dating and relationships from a new direction. Stop letting the fear of getting hurt keep you from experiencing new heights. If you want the exhilaration of flying then you need to be willing to climb up to the top and prepare yourself for take-off. Take some time to think about these concepts and make the necessary changes to become more successful in your relationships.

CHAPTER 7

GIVING AWAY THE POWER

I realize when looking back that I all too often gave away the power in my relationships. I didn't like discord or conflict. I think I was more concerned with achieving and maintaining an idealized, romantic vision of love and harmony. This goal is what I clearly worked for on some crazy unconscious level. The fact that we were doing something together always seemed more important than whether or not it was something I honestly wanted to do. I didn't feel like I was denying myself - I simply didn't put much thought into the terrible imbalance that I was giving life to in my relationships. However, in the end, this method never seemed to pan out. The universal resentment, eventually felt by anyone participating in this type of lopsided relationship dynamic, will always rear its ugly head. This is what I learned.....

Have you ever found yourself giving away the power in your relationships? This concept refers to a pattern of becoming overly focused on your romantic relationships and losing your independence to some degree. Have you found yourself going along with most things and letting someone else make many of the decisions? Do you find relationships to be distracting and have difficulty balancing between your relationships and your own life? This struggle for balance is something that many people can identify with to some degree or another. That balance is crucial to having two independent individuals and one healthy relationship. Let's look at some of the reasons that may lead to "giving away the power" which include a strong desire for a relationship, trouble spreading our mental focus between more than one thing at a time and having difficulty insisting on your own personal boundaries in the emotional realm of love.

Many of us have a strong desire for a healthy relationship. Society has continuously pushed us to believe that we must have one and that it should certainly be one of our main goals. The pull for this relationship can lead to a kind of euphoria when we get it. We may find ourselves simply so happy to be there that we stop interjecting and are focused solely on how nice it all feels. For a time we really may not care about what we do together, just that we are together. When our partners ask us what we want to do over the weekend, we may find ourselves continuously replying, "anything is fine." However, would doing just "anything" with your weekend really be fine if you were single? If not, why lose your sense of person just because you have entered a relationship?

A second reason we may find ourselves "giving away the power" involves our ability to change gears and balance our mental focus and attention. When you are solely focused on another, it is hard to bring mental energy back to our lives and try to distribute it evenly. Sometimes we only feel really "into" someone when we are highly concentrated on him or her. When we then channel energy back to ourselves, it may become confusing as to how strongly we really feel about this person. Take some time to assess if this may be happening in your relationships. Are you having difficulty balancing because anything short of total focus on your partner makes you question the relationship?

The last reason that often contributes to "giving away the power" involves setting personal boundaries. Perhaps you don't really want to be doing everything that you have been doing with your partner. Perhaps you have an excellent ability to set personal boundaries with friends and co-workers but find that you become complacent on this matter in your romantic relationships. However, this inability will lead to eventual resentment, as one cannot maintain this state of imbalance indefinitely. At some point your lack of input may begin to feel too overwhelming to your partner, as they do not always want to always take the lead in the relationship. Assertiveness is attractive, while a lack of assertiveness is not. Additionally, one needs to be able to set boundaries in order to have a personal life of their own. It is essential that each partner develop a personal life with their own interests. When each person is growing and pushing in their personal lives there will always be something new and interesting to bring to the relationship. Without this things can get pretty boring at times as the only thing left to talk about are the mundane routines of the day.

In short, "giving away the power" is not a good recipe for anyone either individually or as a couple. Balance is always the goal in life. Perhaps you have a great ability to balance your life in many ways, but simply have yet to apply this notion to your romantic relationships. Finding this balance will make for a healthier you and a much healthier relationship in the long haul.

CHAPTER 8

THE LOVABILITY FACTOR

I always felt rather unlovable on some level, never really knowing why and actually never really consciously aware of it. I gave and gave, perhaps feeling excess contribution would be the only reason that you needed me around. Again, this feeling was simmering just underneath the conscious, but still clearly there. My repeated attempts at relationships, with people who were utterly emotionally unavailable and quite wounded, really seemed to say everything it needed to. This is what I learned......

Believe it or not, a lot of people suffer silently, or not so silently, with this very thought as it relates to their odds of ever having a successful, long lasting relationship. The scenario often follows a rather clear pattern. You meet, it is exciting and then the ever-reliable anxiety begins to set in. Thoughts such as "why hasn't he called back?", "did I say something wrong?" or "what did he really mean?" now fully consume our mental energy and focus. At this point we start the incessant overanalyzing and it becomes a state from which we cannot escape. The real shame of this expression of anxiety is that we cannot truly be in the present and enjoy the experience. Something that was supposed to be joyful now results in always being on guard and looking for the other shoe to drop. This anxiety in turn works to stifle the natural ease and flow of the relationship and the needed energy which is necessary to build a solid foundation. Therefore, the relationship understandably does not last and unfortunately our original, incorrect message is reinforced, yet again, by another experience. It is time to fight back against this lie we tell ourselves regarding our worthiness to be loved. Instead we need to take a look at three things we can do to begin the climb out of this abyss.

The first thing we can do to fight this lie is to understand that it is just that. It is not real, and there is no real bearing to it what-so-ever. Deep down we may somehow not feel good enough to be worthy of love. Yes, some people have readily identifiable, past events that have understandably affected their self-esteem, and as a result they now feel this way. However, many people find that they feel unlovable, deep inside their core, but they cannot pinpoint a "defining moment" that caused it and cannot understand why this feeling exists at all. Sometimes this feeling can be caused by having felt different all your life, like you never really fit in. Likewise, this feeling can also be attributed to having felt that your presence and feelings have never really mattered. People vary tremendously with their awareness of this feeling. Some individuals are very conscious and quite aware that they somehow feel unlovable, while plenty of others are not consciously aware of it at all. However, people who feel unlovable or "too issue-ridden" often find that they have a pattern of continually choosing emotionally unavailable partners who can't do relationships for the long haul. After all, if you felt better regarding your lovability factor you would insist upon someone who could give you the right kind of love, rather than being scared by it in some way and dismissing those who could actually do so. Understand that the lies we tell ourselves drive the results that we get in our attempts to have successful relationships via the self-fulfilling prophecy. So, stopping the lie is an important first step. It is imperative that we understand this concept.

Now the second thing to do, once you come to accept that you are possibly participating in this lie, is to begin to take real action to fight it. As with most things, we have to work to change the behaviors that are reinforcing it. Low self-esteem is one of the big culprits here in supporting the unworthy factor. It's time to work on building your level of self-esteem by stopping the behaviors that continually cut it down. Once you do, you will no longer default to that original lie. Begin by identifying any of the negative things that you say to yourself on a regular basis. I have always spoken about the immense power of negative self-talk. Derogatory comments about your body image, intelligence or likability need to be put to rest. Identify your personal key negative phrases and write them down. Then, pay attention to when they seem to occur. Does it happen more when you are under stress or interacting with family? If you do see a pattern, try to be especially aware of these times so you can begin to catch yourself more quickly when it does happen. This exercise will help you to understand that the behavior is more likely just something you default to when anxious, rather than having any real basis. Now, get ready with a substitute phrase. This new phrase needs to be a notch up a continuum, not something so unrealistic in comparison to how you actually feel that you simply dismiss the exercise as ridiculous. For instance, if you call yourself fat, as unfortunately so many women do, don't substitute with "I'm the hottest chick this side of the Pecos." That gap is too wide to be helpful. Instead, say something such as, "I'm not quite where I would like to be, but I'm working on it." Getting a handle on your negative self-talk is the first big step you can take towards improving your self-esteem, as that type of behavior keeps you from moving forward.

Finally, if you want to build yourself esteem, start treating yourself in a more loving manner. If you can't treat yourself with love, you probably won't let someone else treat you with love either. So what does it mean to treat yourself in a loving manner? Take an honest assessment of some of the ways in which you may not be acting loving towards yourself. Excess drinking, smoking or sleep deprivation are obvious no brainers. Feeding yourself junk food at the expense of nourishing, life-giving nutrition is another. Do you exercise and move enough or is there improvement that can be made in that area as well? Do you isolate too much or continuously give to others at the expense of yourself? Is it time to think about joining something or finding an activity that, in essence, works to recharge you and fill your energy back up? People have a basic need to be connected, and in our hectic lives, it is essential that we become pro-active in making this happen. If you are not doing that for yourself, then it is time to think about getting started. Practice the art of being good to you. This trial in turn will cause you to attract like energy from someone else and the good stuff will begin to take on a life of its own.

In short, if you find yourself worrying about being lovable, then put the focus back on you. Make an effort to make some changes, and you will find that you feel a world of difference and your self-esteem will noticeably rise. Soon, the idea of being unworthy will melt away like the apparition it is. Work on treating yourself well and your lovability factor will shoot to the moon, assuring that all will work out in the realm of love.

CHAPTER 9

DIFFERENCES

Differences were not something that seemed to be okay in my house growing up. There was one right way to do most things and that was that. So, when I first got into relationships, I sent my partners the very messages that I had received. I really felt that my view of right and wrong was correct. It truly unsettled me that my partner did not see things the way I did when it came to judging people and their behaviors. Only later would I come to understand the truly negative effect this would have on my partners and my relationships. This is what I learned…..

"You're always late," "You take everything too seriously" and "You're never satisfied." Many individuals within a couple find that they are very different from their partners in their approaches to life and their interactions with others. One partner likes to make friends more quickly, while the other likes to move slowly and see if a person can be trusted. One partner enjoys planning things fully, while the other prefers to fly by the seat of his or her pants. One partner feels it is rude to be late, while the other refuses to be a "slave" to time. As a result of these types of personal differences, many couples find that they have repeatedly argued over the same few issues, often for many years, with no real resolve. The greater the dichotomy between partners on certain issues, the greater the chance that arguments to happen. Major differences stem from each partner having separate personal values. These values are shaped by one's life experiences and one's upbringing. Therefore, a person may feel that their very values are being challenged on certain issues, which in turn causes them to cling harder to their way versus compromise. Each partner is fighting to be right. This "right fighting" as it has been termed will drive a relationship to its end if it is not resolved.

The first step in stopping this pattern is to begin to understand that many of the things couples argue over repeatedly are merely the result of differences between the partners. No one is necessarily right or necessarily wrong. Therefore, you must stop insisting that your partner agree with your views. This agreement may never happen. This agreement is not the goal. The goal is to learn to validate the other person's feelings on the matter, regardless of how you feel about it. Additionally, the goal is to find compromise on specific issues, where that is possible. This compromise forces movement towards the middle by both partners. In the middle, each partner feels some sense of validation and equity in having gotten there.

The second step in stopping this pattern is to begin to think about what years of this type of fighting has done or can do to the relationship. This type of fighting often leaves deep wounds in the partners that will need much time to heal. Our values define who we are as a person. Therefore, if we insist on viewing mere differences as right or wrong, we are in essence telling our partner that we do not accept them as they are. We are indirectly telling them that something is wrong with them. However, this behavior is the opposite of love. This is the opposite of what anyone wants from his or her relationship.

If this fighting over differences is happening in your relationship right now, take the time to do something about it. Work with your partner to identify the major issues that you seem unable to resolve. Is there a middle ground where both of you can move to? Not all issues will have a middle ground. Issues involving safety, excessive unhealthy behavior, illegal activity, etc. might fall into this group. However, if there is a middle ground, identify specifics that each partner can do to get there. Work towards achieving a compromise. You are not in this relationship alone and it takes two to do the work. Any problem in the relationship requires the time and attention of both partners. Meeting in the middle is essential for any relationship to survive.

CHAPTER 10

THE VANISHING SELF SYNDROME

When it comes to the idea of losing yourself in a relationship, nobody does it better than I used to. I remember my first, truly significant relationship. I actually had one friend call another friend and say, "We have lost Chris." I had almost literally disappeared. I was not returning calls and was never available, and naturally this worried them. When you don't feel lovable and love finally seems to present itself, it can be intoxicating to the point that you are blinded. You forget about you and the relationship becomes all consuming. And, as is often the case, it becomes toxic like a drug with which you suffer greatly when trying to get off of it. This is what I learned.....

I bet you have seen it in other people's relationships or have participated in it to some degree or another yourself. It is what I like to call the Vanishing Self Syndrome. That place you find yourself in one day, in your relationship, where you have completely neglected your unique individuality and become something else for the supposed sake of the relationship. I have seen this over and over in the course of my couples counseling and it has finally come to a head by the time they enter my office. This Vanishing Self Syndrome is problematic on so many levels that I'm not even sure where to begin. Some of the biggest problems that come to mind include the cessation of personal growth of one of the individuals in the couple, the detrimental effect this type of modeling can have on children and the eventual downfall of the relationship if the balance is not restored at some point.

You have heard me say before that the real beauty of relationships is their potential to facilitate personal growth. The very differences we have with our partners provide a fantastic opportunity to stretch and meet in the middle on those issues with which we are at opposite ends of the spectrum. I know someone who loses herself every time she gets in a relationship. If he likes country music, then she suddenly likes country music, despite no one ever having been aware of this fact prior to her newest relationship. If it just stopped there, with a new passion for a different musical genre it would not be such a big change in her and not such a big deal. However, it never does. She has talked to me about this dynamic that occurs over and over again in her relationships. She allows her friends to go by the wayside and begins to adopt his agenda. It is not that she gets into controlling relationships and is expected to do only what he likes. Instead, it's a pattern gone very wrong. Unfortunately, her personal growth then comes to a halt. At this point her beautiful uniqueness has vanished. This type of configuration results in a great imbalance in their relationship dynamics, and it eventually creates inevitable outcomes. She ends up resentful for having given everything up while still feeling like she isn't getting what she wants. Also, her partners become tired of making all of the decisions and feel highly pressured at the idea of having to be her "everything." She does not have children, but if she did, she would be modeling a very detrimental pattern for them.

A parent's relationship has a profound effect on how a child will formulate ideas, and more importantly, expectations throughout their lifetime. Modeling the Vanishing Self Syndrome to your daughter will have detrimental effects on the quality and duration of her future romantic relationships. The greatest gift we can give our children is to celebrate their beautiful individuality. Encouraging their uniqueness helps to feed their self-esteem and allows them to lead a much more satisfying life, as well as spending a lot less time trying to repair it. When a parental relationship dynamic is way out of balance, most children go on to do one of two things. They either emulate it or go the complete opposite way. If a child emulates the Vanishing Self Syndrome he or she will then continue this pattern. Conversely, he or she may take the direct opposite road, fearing losing themselves like one of their parents, and perhaps have difficulty giving in and compromising on any issue. Either of these scenarios is obviously out of balance and problematic. It is sad not to be able to experience the beauty of a relationship in good harmony with both individuals fully expressing themselves and getting the most out of life.

Lastly, if the Vanishing Self Syndrome exists in any relationship, it will eventually result in its own downfall if it is not addressed and corrected. Nothing in life can sustain itself indefinitely when it is out of balance. It may take years, but eventually the relationship will begin to crumble. And, if it does manage to last, it will most likely be a relationship filled with frequent bickering and resentment.

However, this dynamic can work for quite some time after the relationship has started. Pouring all of that attention and focus onto another can feel good at the beginning and almost like a kind of high. But, in my experience someone will one day eventually and figuratively wake up. At this point this extreme lack of equilibrium will no longer be acceptable for either the one giving up their individuality or for the one on the receiving end of this dynamic. It can be a very hard to transition through the imbalance and restore your relationship to a proper a state of stability.

If this chapter speaks to you, here are several steps you should take. First, sit down with your partner and have an honest discussion about your concerns regarding the state of your relationship. Next, if you are the one neglecting yourself, try to identify some places where you can start to let out your individuality. If you don't really like doing many of the activities you have been going along with during the relationship, start to decrease their frequency.

Making the change will require good communication between the two of you to help this process transition more smoothly. Lastly, get out there and start doing something just for yourself. Take up a new interest or hobby. You may also need professional help to navigate this difficult shift back into equilibrium. Don't hesitate to seek help if you need it. You will feel much better about the relationship and about yourself.

CHAPTER 11

THE ABSENCE OF RESPECT

I found myself particularly sensitive around the topic of respect and what I thought constituted disrespect in my relationships. I was particularly reactionary to tonality, sarcasm, someone telling me to "shut up." I don't like it when people talk poorly to each other and quite frankly will not tolerate it. However, in my early years I put up with way too much, never speaking up due to my lack of voice. I have since tried to find a balance and own my part of the hypersensitivity to the issue. But, I know first-hand the detrimental effects that disrespectful talk can have on a person's self-esteem and sense of well-being. This is what I learned…..

I was talking to a dear friend the other day and she was upset about her sister and brother-in-law's relationship. My friend said that her sister was talking about her husband in such a nasty, disrespectful way that she could hardly stand to be on the phone with her anymore. "What is the problem?," I asked. She proceeded to mention a number of factors her sister was complaining about. While my friend understood her sister's frustration, she was having a hard time with the disrespectful way her sister was characterizing her husband. Most of all, however, she was bothered by the disrespectful way she was talking about him in front of their children. Speaking to your partner in a disrespectful, angry way is very unhealthy and can have many detrimental consequences. This ugly negativism can permanently impact your romantic relationship, your overall sense of well-being and perhaps most importantly your children's lives if it goes unchecked for very long.

The detrimental effect of treating each other with disrespect, on the relationship as a whole, is something I have witnessed first-hand in my practice.

Too often frustration with each other's differences results in sarcastic, angry and disrespectful comments by various partners within the relationship. This dynamic will never work. Yes, some have gone on for years in this state, yet no one is really happy, and it is sad to think of one only getting to have this experience in their short, limited lifetime. Good relationships require a solid foundation. Treating each other with disrespect chips away at the foundation until there is nothing left and eventually the entire relationship collapses. No one deserves to take continual disrespect by his or her partner, and no one should ever treat another in a disrespectful way. This type of dynamic often builds gradually, with a few hurtful comments here and there. However, once this begins, the bar seems to get raised hirer and hirer until it becomes one ugly picture of bad, Jerry Springer type behavior. This level of disrespect is ultimately destructive to not only the relationship, but to your sense of well-being as a whole.

Imagine being belittled and ridiculed for years and years. One can only imagine the damage this type of treatment does to one's self esteem. If you continually hear these negative, abusive comments over and over you may soon begin to tolerate it more and more, you believe it on some level and you may even find yourself beginning to think you deserve it. This progression often occurs in a controlling relationship, as one of the controller's primary objectives is to make you feel like no one else will want you because you are so flawed. Relationships take up quite a bit of your emotional energy when they are not going well. If you are stressed in this area, it is ultimately going to affect just about everything in your life. Work suddenly becomes more stressful and dealing with the children suddenly becomes more stressful, as you have used up so much energy that you just have nothing left to give. Stress leads to depression for some, and in this state your entire outlook is bleak and unhopeful. This is no way to live. Modeling a disrespectful relationship to your children is extremely detrimental to them as well.

Most of us can agree that children are negatively impacted in a relationship where parents treat each other with disrespect. However, we should all take a moment to consider just how intense this impact is and understand all the various ways in which this affects them. Children whose parents fight, argue and speak to each other in a disrespectful way have great damage inflicted on their self-esteem. In many situations they internalize this fighting and somehow begin to think it is their fault. After all, if it is somehow their fault, they can then change this awful thing affecting them that seems to be utterly out of their control. Treating your partner with disrespect affects your children down the road as well, as they go out in the world and begin to choose their mates. Your child may go on to treat their future partners this way and emulate this dysfunctional behavior. On the other hand, although they may not emulate it, your children may instead find themselves continuously gravitating to the familiar and never getting to experience the loving relationship they deserve. At the risk of sounding to Freudian, your early family environment has lifelong impacts on your experiences as an adult.

Treating each other with disrespect is harmful to your relationship, your sense of well-being and most importantly the future lives of your children. If you find yourself in a relationship that is disrespectful, you must gather the courage to insist on doing whatever it takes to change it. The negative impact of living in this kind of situation far outweighs any short-term anxiety you may feel about addressing it.

CHAPTER 12

HUNG UP ON THE "IT"

I distinctly remember agonizing over several early relationships that ended and later wondering what in the hell I had been whining about. At the time I was convinced I needed this relationship and nobody was going to tell me any different. I was "in love" and this person was the one who was going to deliver happily ever after. Naturally, when it ended I was beyond distraught. Then, I came to define the theory of the "it." This is what I learned.....

Have you ever found yourself hung up on the "it"? The "it" refers to that imagined sense of peace and happiness we would feel if we had the relationship of our dreams. It is the beautiful life we imagine creating and sharing with another in a supportive, exciting and comforting relationship. Have you ever found yourself stuck on someone who can't really give you what you need, but you seem to have quite a lot of difficulty letting go? If so, then you are probably hung up on the "it" more than the actual object of your affection. The only problem is that if you stay stuck in that place too long, then you are depriving yourself of the opportunity to experience many of those qualities that you long to share with someone. Being hung up on the wrong person is something that many people have experienced, at some point in their lives, to varying degrees and for varying lengths of time. Three prominent reasons we do this come to mind. It is a safe place to be, it presents a great distracter from your life and it may be a pattern that you simply don't know how to stop.

Do you know someone who has been seemingly "hung up" on somebody else for an extended period of time, despite there being no real chance of having the type of relationship they ultimately desire? Have you ever wondered, "Why are they wasting their time?" Well, they are probably hiding out in a "safe" place. After all, if you remain in this place, then you never really have to go out there and risk having a real relationship that requires doing all of the scary intimacy work associated with it. Staying stuck in this place is simply postponing your chances of experiencing your version of the "it" with someone who is truly capable of giving it to you.

Staying emotionally "hung up" on another also serves as a great distracter from facing and living your own life. If your mind is continuously consumed with fantasies and you are endlessly pining away for another, then you really don't have the focus on yourself. Perhaps you are unhappy with what you have or have not achieved in your life to date and don't know how to move forward. Or, perhaps you have just gone through a particularly rough period and simply need the escape. If you were really focusing on your life, you would have to face the reality that the person you have been "hung up" on simply will not be the one giving you what you want. Endlessly ruminating and trying to answer the "why" questions does not change the fact that it is not working for you.

A final reason for staying stuck may relate to simply not knowing how to break this cycle. It is often human nature for people to think they need answers to something before they can change it. Perhaps you identify with one of the above reasons for staying "hung up" on another or perhaps you don't. However, do you really need this to be answered in order to change it? I say no. Face reality head on and make an honest assessment of the situation. Are you having the great head and heart battle? Do you know in your mind that things won't work, but the pull of your heart seems to keep you stuck? If so then confront things head on. Shake things up a bit and snap yourself out of it. Perhaps you need to make some changes in the level of frequency or duration of time spent with this person, or perhaps you need to have no contact at all. Work to put the focus back on yourself. What short-term and long-term goals have you been putting off lately? Come up with something tangible that you can start today to better your life.

SECTION 2

THE LANGUAGE OF LOVE

CHAPTER 13

INTIMACY

Intimacy has always been something I have craved. No, that is not too strong of a word to describe my feeling. I went through a series of relationships never feeling truly connected to the other person. I always felt that there was something missing. I did not feel understood and I did not feel like my partners shared with me at a level I shared with them. I had issues surrounding sexual intimacy due to things in my past. And, I realized that perhaps I was expecting to get everything from the communication side and did not have a balance going on at the right level in the physical side of the relationship. This is what I learned…..

Intimacy is a broad concept. Couples can be intimate with each other in many different ways. However, I feel that intimacy takes place in two main arenas. These include what I like to call the "communication arena" as well as the "physical arena." A healthy relationship should have a reasonable balance of intimacy invested in these two arenas in order to be successful.

Communication intimacy is the real mainstay of any relationship. It involves vulnerability, as demonstrated by a willingness to risk letting another person know you completely. For example it could include confessing unattractive traits or experiences you've had, which you think might cause him or her to run to Mexico. It involves the willingness to discuss and negotiate the compromises that are necessary in any relationship made up of two people from varying backgrounds. It involves the development of a deep sense of trust and respect that continues to grow throughout a healthy relationship. It involves the acceptance and eventual appreciation of the differences between the two partners. Communication intimacy is the real building block that creates a stable foundation for any relationship. However, too often at the beginning of a relationship all effort to achieve intimacy is placed solely in the physical arena.

Most people have experienced first-hand the problems created when much of the intimacy is placed on the physical side at the expense of the communication side. Have you ever had the initial bliss wear off, only to figuratively wake up and think, "Who is this person?" Additionally, you may suddenly wonder if the person you are dating is even someone you would gravitate towards naturally as a friend. You wouldn't have been so blind-sided if there had been more effort put into the communication side from the start.

Sometimes people have a hard time building intimacy on the communication side. First, it is safer for many people to experience intimacy in the physical arena. You have heard the old saying, "If you really knew me then you might not like me at all." Deep down many people really feel this way. And, rather than risking letting this happen, people often hesitate to share everything they think and feel at the beginning of a new relationship. Therefore, it is safer to put all of the energy toward achieving intimacy into the physical side. Take a serious look at your past dating experiences and ask yourself if this pattern seems vaguely familiar.

Another reason someone may shy away from building communication intimacy is that they simply find it hard to express their feelings. They may have received direct or indirect messages that their feelings did not matter or that it makes someone angry when you state them. Some people stop expressing their feelings altogether because "no one really listens anyway." Partners in healthy relationships work to create an atmosphere where each partner feels heard and validated. If you don't, you will never really know the person sitting across from you.

CHAPTER 14

BOUNDARIES

I always had what thought was a good understanding of the concept of boundaries. Perhaps they were too good, or better yet too rigid. Not the type of rigidity that comes from being controlling, rather the type that attempts to protect oneself from the unexpected and unpleasantness in the world that no one can truly, fully escape. I have worked hard to move from a personality that naturally gravitates to a world defined in black and white, to one that is seen in more moderate shades of gray. I was trapped in a box, trying to protect myself from the world by anticipating all that could go wrong and avoiding situations that could "obviously" be foreseen. I wanted you to live in that same box as well. Fortunately, I have mellowed and relaxed this trait with age. This is what I learned.....

Boundaries define who an individual is as a person. Boundaries reflect our values, our likes and dislikes, and most importantly, how we expect to be treated by others. Boundaries are also used to define our needs. For example, some people need more "down time" than others, and some people need more social interaction than others. When we enter relationships, we each have different needs. Stating our individual needs and seeing that they are met requires setting clear, strong boundaries within the relationship. However, proficiency at this skill often takes a good deal of practice.

For example, suppose you have had a terrible day at work and decide you need to stay home that night and take care of yourself. However, your partner gets home and really wants you to go out to dinner. The person with clear, strong boundaries is better able to state their need to stay home and rest. However, the person with less strong boundaries consistently finds himself or herself doing things that they may not really want to do. This person does not have a healthy boundary between their individual self and the relationship. The balance between "I" and "we" is something that all relationships struggle to achieve. Healthy relationships have achieved this balance. In these relationships, the partners see themselves as both individuals with differing needs and as part of a couple. They are better able to set the necessary boundaries to differentiate between these two.

In addition to having clear individual boundaries, a healthy relationship must also have clear relationship boundaries set around the couple itself. If you value what you have in your home, you lock your door at night. You have clearly set a boundary for those who might intrude. Well, if you value your partner and your relationship, why not set healthy boundaries around it too. Let others know that you are a couple and that you are happy. Reinforce this union by allowing natural demonstrations of affection to take place in front of friends. It works to identify the two of you as a couple. You now have set a boundary by drawing an imaginary line around your relationship. It then becomes clear if someone tries to cross it.

You should also understand that you will need to set boundaries differently with different people. Take a good look at the people in your lives. Do they respect boundaries? Do they understand what boundaries are? If they don't, feel free to educate them. This applies to your friends, but especially to your partner. If you don't insist that your boundaries be respected, then why should anyone else?

CHAPTER 15

INSECURITY

Wow, I certainly could have been a poster child for insecurity and all of the awful feelings that accompany it. No, I didn't act like a jealous loon and cause problems in the relationship in a negative way. Instead, I silently suffered with feelings of anxiety whenever new "friends" suddenly entered the picture and began to become too large a part of my partner's lives. I didn't understand that this insecurity was heightened by the fact that I suffered from low self-esteem and the partners I chose were the unavailable type who needed to start up something emotionally with someone else while in a relationship. This is what I learned…..

Many people have experienced infidelity and/ or other feelings of betrayal in their relationships throughout the years. Someone who has been cheated on in a previous relationship will understandably and inevitably carry some baggage of insecurity along with the subsequent jealousy that comes with it. However, this feeling of anxiety is something that often cannot be solved on an individual basis alone and needs to be worked out in the context of a relationship. After all, these feelings are not going to flare up when you are single. Unfortunately, most couples do not know how to handle feelings of insecurity when they exist in one or more of the partners. Life happens to us all. The feelings we have been left with from life's experiences are not the real problem. Rather, it is how we choose or choose not to deal with them that are the real issue. It is imperative for people to understand that they must pull their baggage out, set it on the table and deal with it if they want to have successful relationships. However, level of vulnerability can be very hard for many of us to do because we feel ashamed for having these feelings.

I have spoken with individuals who share surprisingly similar stories regarding their feelings of insecurity when in a relationship. If you have ever suffered from these anxiety producing thoughts you are not alone. "I feel threatened when my partner meets someone new and starts talking about them a lot," is something that I hear in therapy sessions. People often feel ashamed of having these feelings because their partners are not actually doing anything over the line by all appearances. And, if they do express their concerns, they are often met with such lovely words as "neurotic" or "insecure." After all, the partner knows that he or she is not up to anything and therefore thinks that the feelings of jealousy and insecurity are not warranted by their loved one. It is exactly at this point that partners get completely off track and start accusing each other of being right or wrong. This negative reaction explains why the person who experiences this type of insecurity has learned to spend much time silently suffering, as they have received the message that it is wrong to feel this way and therefore they must keep this deep, dark secret to themselves. Treating these feelings like something shameful, which must be banished back behind closed doors, will never alleviate this situation. Instead the goal is to create a safe and secure environment in your relationship where you feel comfortable throwing this baggage out on the table. After all, the ability to do just this is what equates to true intimacy.

Feelings of insecurity often stem from some fairly predictable origins. First, you may have actually experienced an infidelity in one of your past relationships and have been left with some justifiable trust issues. Second, you may be suffering from low self-esteem. A new person suddenly entering the mix can feel threatening because they might be so charismatic, interesting or appealing that your partner could not help but be drawn to them. However, if you are thinking this way you are forgetting about all of the wonderful qualities that drew your partner to you in the first place. You are viewing yourself as so insignificant that you could be that easily forgotten. Lastly, your partner may be unknowingly walking a little too close to the boundary line in their interactions with others. Therefore, the logic of your thoughts, coupled with heightened perceptions, has hijacked your emotions and is taking over. The more you deny these feelings, the more they will intensely grip you. This is the universal law that applies to "baggage." If you suffer from feelings of insecurity, it is your job to bring this topic up in your relationship.

Is it your partner's job to solve your baggage? No, but if two people truly care for one another and are interested in making the relationship work, they must work together. Everyone has issues to work through and it is never completely one-sided. Explain to your partner that insecurity is something you struggle with and identify the past experiences that you think have contributed to these feelings. Have a lengthy discussion on boundaries and make suggestions to your partner about what changes may be helpful to increase your feelings of security in the relationship. Setting good clear boundaries around the two of you as a couple will go a long way to alleviate some of your tension.

CHAPTER 16

PATTERNS

Patterns can at once be great tools for learning and unbelievably frustrating. We've all heard that saying about the definition of insanity described as continually doing the same thing and expecting different results. Unfortunately, repeating patterns is just what I did in relationships. I think that the heightened emotionality that accompanies relationships makes it harder to step outside yourself and see non-productive patterns in both who you choose and how you behave in relationships. However, it is these very patterns that keep you stuck and unfulfilled in love. This is what I learned......

I wrote a Relationship Coaching Workbook which I designed to help people stop cycling in and out of unsuccessful relationships. One of the exercises in this workbook involves a section on patterns. I help clients to identify their choice patterns and behavior patterns when it comes to their romantic relationships. I ask them to think back on all of their past relationships and look for commonalities among the individuals they have chosen to pursue. Some people are drawn to partners who are controlling, emotionally unavailable, drink too much, can't commit, have bad tempers and such. I refer to this as their choice patterns. I also ask them to identify patterns in the ways they have ended up feeling or behaving throughout many of their different relationships. This I refer to as their behavior patterns. Our particular patterns speak to us, not our blind luck in repeatedly choosing the same situation and getting the same tired results. Two steps are required to change your patterns. You must first identify them and then you must take action to change them. Perhaps the discovery of one of my key patterns will help to illustrate this point.

I have tried to work hard through the years to identify my own behavior patterns and make the necessary changes to end that cycle. I was that person who repeatedly gave 120% in my relationships and always ended up feeling used, unappreciated and taken for granted. I went to therapy myself, and it was sometimes hard to accept any perceived lack of capability. I prided myself on having a good ability to identify my own crap and fix the situation. It was difficult for me to swallow the fact that I was actually creating that feeling of not being appreciated and being taken for granted. I found it to be both a humbling journey and a liberating one. So, once I brushed off my bruised ego and accepted this fact, I had to find out why I was giving so much. For me it came down to pure self-esteem. It was as if I would be loved only for the deeds I did, rather than for the good person I wanted to believe myself to be. I was in essence discounting all of my positive qualities which ten years ago I would not have even been able to state. Instead, I spent too much time focusing on the qualities I thought were wrong with me and never gave myself the chance to learn to feel really good about myself. Hence, the pattern was reinforced. So, how did I work to change all of this? I decided to take action.

I tell all of my clients that I am an action-oriented type of therapist. In other words, I am all about putting some behavioral changes in place to try to rectify the current pattern once it is identified. If I suffered from giving too much, I was simply going to have to pull back. After all, it really wasn't rocket science was it? I became elated that I now knew what had to be done to change this pattern for myself. I tried to pay attention to my thoughts. Every time I found myself wanting to do something to go that extra mile in my relationship, I would simply pull back and tell myself no about 50% of the time. Well, that sounds great in theory. However, nobody told me the wrath of emotions that would come pouring out of the floodgates when I decided to implement pulling back in these identified areas. Every time I pulled back from giving too much, I felt great angst and unease, as if my excess giving was the glue that had been holding the entire relationship together and now it was going to come crashing down like a house of cards. Pulling back somehow seemed like the antithesis of a loving act, and I struggled greatly to force myself to do something that felt like this to me. Did I really think on an intellectual level that this feeling was rational? No, but I have always been a little too ruled by my emotions and it seemed to be overpowering my brain. I was changing the pattern of interactions in my relationship and I was not naïve enough to think that there wouldn't be reverberations on the other side. My partner started reacting to my pulling back, which in turn made it harder for me to continue the new behaviors I was trying to implement. I knew I had to tolerate these reverberations. Otherwise, I would not persevere in changing the uneven dynamics of giving in my relationship and ultimately my accompanying feelings of being taken for granted.

I'm happy to say that I have become much better about not bringing this pattern into my more recent relationships. However, I have to think consciously about my old pattern from the very start and take steps to not go there. I am a giver by nature. I don't think I will ever be in some 50/50 type of situation when it comes to giving. I may always be the 65% type of girl. However, at that level I don't create the negative feelings for myself and more importantly I allow room for someone to give to me. After all, is that not what I was really wanting all along? Engaging in my previous pattern was not only making me feel bad, but also it was actually keeping me from getting what I had always wanted: someone who was giving to me. I realized that I was not comfortable letting someone give to me. Being the receiver of giving had never been my role, the role I so perfectly emulated from watching my mother while growing up. That behavior had always made me so sad and many times frustrated that my mother did not know how to let others give to her. Wow, I was doing the same thing. My detrimental pattern of giving 120% had been keeping me safe from the uncomfortable situation of receiving.

In short, our patterns need to be identified and action needs to take place. Equally important, you need to be able to tolerate the predictable reverberations you will get from your partner when you change the dynamics in your relationship by taking action. Behavior patterns can be changed, and with these changes you will find yourself and your relationship doing much better in the long run.

CHAPTER 17

VULNERABILITY

My walls to vulnerability began as a child who was either told, or it had been implied, that I was "too sensitive." Emotionality was not displayed in my house. I don't recall people saying things like, "that hurt my feelings" or "you really scared me when you did that." Unfortunately early on I formed the message that it was somehow not okay to have my feelings. They would not be recognized as valid or legitimate by the rest of the world. As a result, I was not able to let other people know when I was upset or hurt by something they had said or done. Oh sure, I could blow up like everybody else. However, I could not be vulnerable enough to say how I felt and therefore never really had the intimate, fully connected relationships that I had so craved. This is what I learned.....

Vulnerability is to intimacy as water is to fish. You can't have one without the other. Vulnerability equals risk. Risk is scary because there is no guarantee that relationships will last or turn out to be what we imagine. Matters of the heart are highly emotional and can produce quite a bit of pain and discomfort. Risk is what is necessary to push through the fear, rather than letting it paralyze your designs for a successful life. Therefore, one must push oneself to be vulnerable (risk) in order to gain ever-increasing levels of intimacy in a relationship. Vulnerability is what feeds relationships so they continue to grow rather than wither and die.

I have referred many times to the two arenas of intimacy. These arenas include the communication arena and the physical arena. While both afford their own unique opportunity for varying types of vulnerability, the real "glue" of the relationship occurs in the communications. Talking and sharing feelings provides the opportunity for real emotional vulnerability to take place. The idea of letting another know you completely feels both risky and scary in the context of a romantic situation. Many of us find fault within ourselves. In actuality, many of us are almost brutal with the negative self-talk in which we engage. Our negative self-perceptions, often far worse in thought than actuality, are not exactly something that we are particularly eager to divulge to someone with whom we are romantically attracted. Why? Because this act requires that we open up and expose ourselves. The fear and anxiety that this exposure produces can at times feel overwhelming, and we tend to retreat in order to protect ourselves. This feeling and subsequent behavior is fairly universal. It only becomes problematic if one does not consciously make an effort to push through the fear and remain present.

Fear and discomfort do not kill you. They are simply unpleasant feelings. The absence of fear is never the goal. The goal is to tolerate the fear, eventually accept its presence in your life and push on despite. Do not make the mistake of designing a life void of fear and uncomfortable situations. If you do, you will cease to grow and will miss out on the bountiful rewards on the other side of that fear. Fear accompanies the unknown. If you have not had any unknown for a while, you could be guilty of complete and total stagnation. All success in life involves coping with fear and pushing through its grip. That evolution results in advancement. The process of growth can seem painful at times, but there is often something very rewarding at the other end of the struggle.

In relationships we need to push ourselves to admit our flaws, fears, insecurities or other items with which we often associate shame. The beauty of vulnerability is that we open up and let this garbage out. We can free ourselves of this self-imposed noose. This freedom and subsequent feelings of acceptance by our partner is the real prize of intimate romantic relationships. When we allow ourselves to dip into the pool of intimacy we find that there exists a direct, proportional relationship between our ability to be vulnerable and the degree of healing that takes place. However, this result is only experienced if we can muster up the courage to reap this reward. The choice is yours. Take advantage of the healing opportunities that are only magnified in the context of safe and respectful romantic relationship.

CHAPTER 18

UNMET NEEDS

My needs were something, I'm embarrassed to say, that were never really even considered in my early relationships. Gee, I wonder why they never worked out. I guess it goes back to that lacking sense of self-esteem. I was always getting picked and never really doing the picking. This pattern was clearly, although unknown to me at the time, a perfect way to avoid rejection. You like me and I want a relationship. I suppose I was happy just to have a relationship and the idea that I would need certain things to be happy quite frankly never occurred to me. Since I wouldn't have put up with being treated poorly, I must have thought that I had already done my part. This is what I learned…..

Unmet needs. Simply put, this void is the number one reason that individuals are unhappy in their current relationships. In my relationship coaching sessions, clients are asked to write a "wants & needs" list. I always tell them that if they ever feel unhappy in future relationships, they should pull that list out and I guarantee that one of their "needs" is not being met by their partner. The benefit of completing this exercise is that they can quickly identify which one it is because they already have the list. Better yet, they can show the list to potential partners in the early stages of dating. It is essential that your individual needs are met in a relationship if it is to run smoothly and bring you comfort. Several prominent reasons contribute to the end result of not getting one's needs met in romantic relationships. These include not being able to clearly articulate these needs, treating our partner the way we want to be treated (rather than how they want to be treated) and that we simply have never had a conversation about needs with our partner.

Being able to communicate your needs is a must in relationships. When clients come to my office, they often state their unhappiness in broad terms. "I don't feel loved" or "I'm not appreciated," are common declarations. Yes, while we can all probably identify with those feelings, they are not specific enough. I asked, "What does that mean?" I want to know what would be happening that would make you feel loved. For some that might include having your partner leave sweet little notes or flowers, actions that let you know the other person was thinking of you, and for others that could mean someone asking how your day went on a regular basis and greeting you with hugs at the door. It is so natural for us to default to what is wrong with the other person, rather than learning to say what it is we need.

Another reason we don't get our needs met is that many of us tend to give to the other person in the way that we would like someone to give back to us. For instance, I want a big hug when I am upset with something in the world, and I want to talk about it right now. This is the action that makes me feel better. However, many people don't like to be touched when they are upset and want to wait until they feel less charged to have a conversation about something that happened to them at the office. As I have always said this is a matter of differences. In a relationship we need to ask our partners what they need when they are upset, rather than to continue to give to them in a way that we would like back. This dynamic creates a fundamental problem in many relationships, learning to see our partners for who they are and what they need.

Lastly, most couples have never really sat down and talked about their needs with each other. If they did, then the dynamics would run a lot more smoothly. That is what you do in a relationship. You do things for the other person "just because." It doesn't matter that you don't need a particular something. Perhaps your partner does. You likewise will have needs that he or she doesn't have. This process of discovery is the beauty of learning someone in a relationship. People can clearly articulate when they are unhappy, but they need to be able to state what they need as well. A woman came to my office and stated that she didn't feel appreciated. I asked her what he could be doing that would make her feel appreciated. She said that she wasn't sure. I asked, "Well, how in the world is he supposed to know if you don't even know?" People are not mind readers. Stop expecting that from your partner.

In short, unmet needs equates to unhappiness in relationships. Take some time to sit down and write your needs on a piece of paper. Some of these needs will be the direct opposite of what you did or didn't get in past relationships. Therefore, certain needs will be tailored to you specifically, while there are certain universal needs that must be met in all relationships in order for the individuals to be happy. These would include the need for someone who is willing or able to compromise and willing or able to push themselves to open up and be vulnerable. Only when you can clearly articulate your needs will you be able to see the person standing right in front of you who can actually meet them.

CHAPTER 19

HOW TO EXPRESS
YOUR FEELINGS

In my early relationships I found myself with no voice. I suffered from a low lovability factor. I had also experienced parents who argued a lot. Therefore, I had formed a strong belief, very early on, that people who love each other don't fight. So, conflict, or the idea of it, was something that I avoided like the plague. I would sit and suffer silently when my feelings were hurt by something my partners either said or did. Inevitably, at some future date, I would explode and overreact to something seemingly benign because something new would happen and resonate with the old, unexpressed hurt. Naturally, nothing got resolved and I never felt understood. How could I? I didn't know how to express my feelings. This is what I learned…..

When we suddenly become upset it is as if we have become almost "emotionally hi-jacked." This is not the time to try to convey to your partner what you are feeling. It will invariably come out jumbled, fragmented and probably in a non-productive tone of voice. As a result, your partner will probably become defensive and at a minimum will not be able to hear you. Delivery is everything. I do not feel that anger is really a legitimate emotion in and of itself. The question is, "what is really behind the anger"? When we are mad, we can almost always trace this feeling to another level. We are hurt or we are afraid.

People get feelings hurt for a wide variety of reasons. These emotions often revolve around themes such as disrespect, inconsideration or feeling taken for granted just to name a few. Many of the times we are mad at our partners, you can bet that their words or actions have ignited one of these feelings of hurt. It is essential that you clearly identify why you are upset. On the other hand, we often get upset when we are afraid. Fear tends to revolve around common themes as well such as thoughts of abandonment, issues of safety or projections of things to come based on previous relationship experiences. If you suddenly find yourself emotionally hijacked, what should you do about it?

First, take a time-out. Tell your partner that you are feeling really upset and that you need some time to figure out exactly where it is coming from. However, always state when you will return to the discussion. It is maddening to be dismissed with no understanding of when the situation might get resolved. Therefore, always provide a time such as in a half an hour or tonight after work. Then, ask yourself why you are upset. Have your partner's actions or words hurt your feelings or made you afraid in any way? It is essential that you learn to identify your feelings accurately if you want your partner to hear you and you want to be validated. Also, take an honest assessment of why your reaction was so heightened. Would everyone you know have been as upset as you from what transpired, or did this incident flare up particular hot buttons or sensitivity around this particular topic? If so, then you need to own that, as it is unfair to assign all of that level of upset to your partner. Usually one of three actions has occurred. Your partner was totally out of line, your old tapes flared up because the issue zinged one of your hot buttons or it could be a combination of both. Take the time to try and assess which action has taken place so you can convey this to your partner. Lastly, go back to the table. Ask your partner to listen to you for a few minutes and not to interrupt. Calmly tell your partner the real reason you think you got upset, own up to your part in the heightened emotions and explain what you need your partner to differently in the future regarding this topic.

If you both work to implement this technique you will finally begin to hear each other and think about how your actions affect your partner. This exercise also has the great benefit of working to develop real intimacy in your relationship. You begin to truly understand each other, how you view the world and what you feel strongly about. Someone telling me they are mad at me tells me absolutely nothing about them. Breaking it down let's me into the world of their feelings and helps me to feel that much more connected.

SECTION 3

DOING THINGS DIFFERENTLY

CHAPTER 20

JUDGING RELATIONSHIP POTENTIAL

Early on I simply followed the heart from one bad relationship to the next. The heart can be a pretty powerful driver and often seemed to get in the way of all rational thought for me when it came to relationships. Early on I never looked at love from the stand point of how do I get what I want and need from a relationship. This is what I learned…..

"How do I know if this person is the one?" I'm often asked. This question is single- handedly the most commonly asked relationship related dilemma that everyone wants answered. Unfortunately, no definitive test or magical combination of characteristics that will alleviate the fear and risk that many of us feel when entering into a new relationship. I have often referred to myself as a hopeless romantic. However, I do not believe in the concept of "the one." There are many individuals with whom we can have a successful relationship. Those people you admire who currently possess a long lasting, healthy relationship do not do so because they found the needle in the haystack. Potentially healthy relationships exist for all and are waiting to be had. Nevertheless, certain relationship characteristics must be present if a relationship is to have any real chance at a favorable outcome.

All too often, people are focused on common interests as the main measure for potential in a new relationship. However, I could line up 10 people with the same interests and that commonality does not mean that they are necessarily capable of having a flourishing relationship. Your ability to communicate as a couple far surpasses any other characteristic as the best gauge of the relationship's chances for survival and happiness. Communication is the key. The ability to tolerate, negotiate and eventually accept each other's differences is another key indicator of a relationship's potential. Therefore, once the differences are acknowledged, both partners must show willingness to compromise for the sake of the relationship. The ability to bring up and deal with uncomfortable topics in a safe and respectful manner is another big indicator of the relationship's potential for longevity. A relationship cannot thrive if either partner is afraid to discuss how he or she is being affected by the other partner's behavior.

If you have just started dating, then you have the perfect opportunity to develop your internal gauge for measuring a relationship's potential. We all operate in la la land when we first enter a new relationship. Wake up! Start paying attention early on to the flexibility of the person you are dating. If you are dating someone who repeatedly says, "This is how I am...take it or leave it," you had better leave it. Nothing is wrong with someone who doesn't want to change. However, this person should remain single because this type of inflexibility will never work for the person who wants a happy and fulfilling relationship. If in hindsight your date said something that did not set well with you, bring it up. Don't be afraid to rock the boat. Let's find out early on how your date does with honest questioning and possible differing of opinions. Also, how does your date do with compromise? Are you always going to your date's house and him or her rarely going to yours? Are you always doing what your date wants and not what you want? Express your feelings early on. How does your date handle your emotions? Are they validated and acknowledged? The ability of your partner to do this is essential if a relationship is to have any real promise. Again, communication is the key. Focus on these actions at the beginning and save yourself a lot of wasted time if it is not happening.

CHAPTER 21

WALKING THROUGH
THE DOOR OF "NO"

The idea of walking through the "door of no" was something that was not even remotely in my conscious thoughts. After all, I had never left any relationship in the past, no matter how bad or how unfulfilling. I had such an insatiable yearning to be loved, to try and fill that never-ending, empty hole of loneliness and feelings of unlovability. The idea that one would leave a relationship, just because they weren't getting their needs met, was utterly foreign and completely removed from my realm of possibilities. This is what I learned.......

I have heard much talk these days about manifesting your dreams through the "Law of Attraction". Many books are available that teach you how to create your ideal life and many CD's exist to help you meditate to that place. I personally think that all of these venues are valuable in that they provide an avenue to put forth positive energy to help you get out of your own way and push forward towards your goals. After all, I do believe that the only thing between you and your dreams is you. The act of getting out of your own way means learning to state a firm and resounding "no" to something that will not meet your needs. So, while many tools are helpful, you need to proceed to your big life through the "door of no". When it comes to getting the relationship you so crave, you must stop wasting time in relationships that can't meet your needs. I strongly believe that until you can master walking through the door of no, and leaving things that aren't working, then and only then have you properly freed up your energy to go forth and design your life in your terms of success. In order to be able to walk through the door of no, you have to practice developing your faith in life, learn to tolerate the fear of the unknown and

set firm boundaries for yourself while seeing that
you respect them.

I have talked before about faith. I am referring to
a belief that something can be so, without any proof to
back that assumption up. Many people have lost their
faith in the idea of having a good solid relationship.
This nagging doubt has usually been backed up with
bad experiences or having thus far experienced a
seemingly endless stream of relationships that were
headed nowhere. So, I'm not questioning the logic
of your feeling that way. However, I'm asking you
to be willing to set that conviction aside and work
to restore your faith by putting action into place
rather than listening to your negative thoughts.
You have heard the saying "fake it until you make it."
Well, that premise is just where you need to start.
You need to learn to trust that a great relationship will
not just happen. It will only come on the other side
of having learned to say no, and then actually
experiencing walking away from something that

you know in your heart will not make you happy. Yes, it may seem as if the faith needs to be present first in order to be strong enough to take that action, yet I believe that the act of taking care of yourself in this manor ultimately builds your faith. You have to begin to trust that this is true even though you have no proof. You proof will only come once you have crossed the threshold of the door of no.

Being able to tolerate the fear of the unknown is an adult life skill that we all need to master. With respect to relationships, it is this very problem that keeps us in hopeless marriages and unhappy relationships. We fear that we may never find another relationship. We fear that we may find something far worse. We fear that everyone will hate us and stop talking to us if we leave. This fear creates a great paralysis and is the very reason that we stay stuck in our relationships, our unsatisfying jobs and all the other areas of life where we are missing out on forward progress. Facing the unknown, by consciously and actively putting yourself in its presence is the only way to master the fear. Once we realize that the world didn't come to an end and that we still have our home and job, we can start to become de-sensitized to this gripping fear. It would be nice if we had the faith prior to the walk, but is the act of walking that helps develop the faith that everything will work out. And, as we develop this faith, it becomes easier and easier to set the necessary boundaries to get what we want.

The boundaries we set with other people are in essence boundaries that we are setting for ourselves. They most often pertain to what we will and won't tolerate. We won't put up with the dog going to the bathroom inside the house. We won't put up with someone driving their car over our garden. We have no problem setting those obvious boundaries. So, why do people struggle so much with setting personal boundaries that pertain to how we let others treat us and ultimately waste so much time in relationships that are going nowhere? We do this battling because we lack the faith that something good is coming around the bend. We want the guarantee in order to stand up for ourselves. If I promised you that a fantastic relationship was waiting in the wings, if the current one didn't work out, you would have a much easier time setting appropriate boundaries and saying, "this behavior needs to change or I am out of here". That guarantee would give you the confidence and rise in self-esteem to listen to your instincts and make the right choice. But, we don't get the guarantee in life. We simply have to learn to hold our head up high and keep moving forward in search of what we desire, never settling for less. Doing so equates to the ultimate responsibility we need to set and keep for ourselves. That accomplishment is the path to experiencing greater and greater heights in love, intimacy, career or anything else. And, if you do find you have to set the appropriate boundaries and move on, don't waste your time viewing it as a failed relationship.

Instead of ruminating on a sense of failure spend some time reflecting on what it was you were supposed to learn so you don't repeat that same scenario. We are all learning and gathering in order to gain great clarity on what we need to be happy and to recognize the person who can ultimately meet those needs. Learning to set good boundaries for ourselves and leave when it is not working not only demonstrates great self-care, but also it sends you on your journey through the door of no. Learn to walk across the threshold, and the world will begin to reward you with sweet surprises just waiting on the other side.

CHAPTER 22

HOW TO GET OFF THE FENCE

Wow, for the overly analytical mind, coupled with a touch of anxiety, learning how to become more decisive about staying or going is essential for one's state of mental health. That great head and heart battle between your rational and emotional side can really wreak havoc on your peace of mind. I have always had a great ability to be able to justify just about anything, within reason, that I really want. But, this trait isn't always a good thing when it pertains to relationships. For years I couldn't even get on the fence. However, once I did, I found it extremely difficult to move to one side or the other. This is what I learned.......

When is it time to move on? When is it time to dig in and try harder? How many times have you been at this crossroads before in your current relationship? Figuring out where to go from this juncture is hard stuff and involves hard choices. This question is one that I get asked over and over, as a therapist, from people coming into my office for answers to this dilemma. Although life is never that black and white in reality, here are a few basics to think about that may help you learn how to get off of the fence. These include an honest assessment of the following: your partner's willingness to work with you to make things better, your partner's ability to actually meet your needs and your ability to be forthright with yourself as to why you might really be staying in the relationship.

If you have been unhappy in your relationship and have seen the problems, it is time to ask yourself what you've done to try to make it better. New clients have come to my office upset because despite asking, their partners are unwilling to come to couples counseling. It is at this point that you need to insist. In other words, tell your partner that you are worried that the relationship is spiraling downward. Let them know that you feel the two of you need help and that if they don't agree to go, you are very concerned about the inevitable ending. After all, something totally out of balance cannot maintain itself in that state indefinitely. If you let them know your fears and they still refuse to participate, you will be able to leave the relationship knowing that you did everything you could. Make sure that you take this step and you won't have to go through the tortuous "should have," "could have" game in your head after the relationship ends.

A second factor to consider when deciding to stay or go involves stepping back and taking an honest look at your relationship. Is it possible that two good people have hooked up but just aren't really right for each other? Many times this scenario is the case but no one in the relationship really wants to see it or admit that possibility to themselves.

Are you trying to get your needs met from someone who can't meet them? In the process are both of you wounding each other with constant criticisms of the other's lack of action? Plenty of people come to realize that they were trying to force something that was not really coming that naturally. We all have to make some changes in order to have a relationship run smoothly, as you are not dating yourself and the natural differences will have to be negotiated. However, if it is constant work, it is possible that you may not be right together, and that premise can be a very difficult one to accept.

Lastly, in trying to get off the fence, you need to assess all the possible reasons that you might actually be hanging on. Very common reasons exist as to why people choose to stay in relationships that are not working. People stay because they are terrified at the idea of hurting another and don't feel they can handle the guilt, which is always present if you are the "leaver" in the relationship and certainly compounded if children are involved. Unfortunately, people also stay because they tell themselves that "something is better than nothing." I can't tell you how many times I've heard someone complaining about the idea of having to get back out there in the dating world. Simultaneously, great fears abound regarding being able to ever find anyone again for a relationship. While these are logical and understandable statements, it does not mean that these suspicions are true. It is simply a reflection of the level of fear associated with taking such a big step. Moving forward is often scary and often hard to do.

In short, at some point you will have to decide to get off the fence. Ask your partner to participate in fixing the relationship and making it better. If they don't, you will finally be able to exit with a sense of peace about the matter, as you have done all that you can. Ask yourself if the two of you are really right for each other. Lastly, ask yourself if you're staying for the right reasons and not out of fear. Taking the time to ask and answer these questions will help you to get off of the fence and get on with life one way or another.

CHAPTER 23

LEAVING WITH INTEGRITY

I had an obvious pattern attached to the ending of my relationships until the more recent years. I was always the one left, and I was always deeply hurt and extremely angry. The victimization theme came crashing at me with full force, whether the break up was ultimately for the best or not. I didn't like feeling victimized, I just didn't know how to see things from any other perspective. "Why," I ruminated, "did no one want to love me?" I came to realize that the only reason I was always left was that I would never leave when I should have. Therefore I set the stage for this pattern, and accompanying anguish, over and over again. I would still stay connected after it ended, sending my emotions on an ever exhausting roller coaster to nowhere. Eventually, I learned to leave and had to put the shoe on the other foot. This is what I learned.....

The way in which one chooses to leave a relationship ultimately says a lot about one's character and one's level of integrity. Endings are almost never neat, clean or perfect. Understandable, reactionary anger from the one being left in turn fuels guilt on many levels for the one who chooses to leave. Let's face it, it's tough to be left; but it is also very tough to leave someone you once loved. People are looking for almost anything to make themselves feel better or forget the inevitable guilt they experience when taking on this position in the ending of their relationship. Unfortunately, far too often individuals finally muster up the courage to leave after they have found someone else to start seeing, which in turn hurts the one being left on an even greater level. So, the question then becomes, "How do you leave a relationship with integrity?" Key elements include: making sure you leave prior to involving another person, making sure that you fairly and quickly enact the painful division of property and making sure that you set clear boundaries with your ex so the healing process can begin.

Perhaps you have taken the easy way out at the ending of past relationships. Perhaps you were too afraid to hurt your partner so you instead, unconsciously waited for someone else to come along to remind yourself that there really could be more compatibility in relationships. Although cheating on someone either physically or emotionally is quite painful for the person on the other end, it is important to understand why this phenomenon so often happens at the end of relationships. Many well intentioned individuals get together and later discover that they are with someone who simply cannot meet their needs and is too incompatible. Then, inevitably, another person comes along who reminds you of all those qualities you've been missing. It is at this moment that one figuratively "wakes up", realizes that the original connection is virtually nonexistent and begins the emotional or physical entwinement with the new person. However, this is what I like to call taking the "easy way out". It is easy because you have avoided all the hard steps which are involved in the process of coming to terms with the fact that a particular relationship will not work and then taking the necessary action to match that conclusion. These steps include being brutally honest with yourself along the way as to the state of your relationship, facing possible rejection by bringing up the relationship problems to see if you can get cooperation to fix them and ultimately, making the conscious decision to leave when you knew that the relationship was not going to work. If you can relate to this synopsis do not feel bad or feel judged, as we all need some work on how to leave a relationship with integrity. I am simply stating that it would be best to rise to the occasion and try to improve the way that you leave relationships in the future. You will feel better about yourself and it won't hurt nearly as badly for your partner.

A second way we can leave with integrity involves setting emotions aside and being as equitable as possible with regards to tying up the loose ends and divvying up the physical stuff. Let the tit-for-tat behavior take a back seat to your sanity and don't do anything to drag the process out. Get your things out of the house and do it soon. Don't fool yourself into thinking you can't get it all, when what you may actually be doing is creating a reason to stay connected, if even on an unconscious level. The ending of a relationship is like a death on many levels. It is the ending of the familiarity which accompanies living day in and day out with someone you once loved. It is the death of all the hopes and dreams you had for what the two of you might share together. You've seen how ugly people can get over money when someone has died. Well, relationships can get pretty ugly too. Emotions are running at their peak. You can choose to make the procedure much easier on the both of you by setting emotions aside, playing fair and making a clean break of things as soon as possible.

Lastly, leaving with integrity involves setting clear boundaries as to what future interaction is going to look like between the two of you. It is different for everyone. Some people remain friends and some don't. There is no perfect blueprint for how to end a relationship. However, I am a firm believer that it is necessary for all involved parties to have a healthy period of respite regardless of the ultimate outcome regarding friendship. Unfortunately, the person who leaves often wants to remain friends on some level. It is understandable, as the idea of never again seeing someone he or she spent so much time with is rather unbearable. But, without a reasonable break the new, raw emotions run wild and the roller coaster ride often proves to be too much for both parties. Therefore, understand that staying in contact will prevent your ex from beginning the healing process. Your need for reassurance from a continued connection of some kind, just to alleviate fears of never seeing he or she again, is not helpful for either party involved. You've done what you needed to do for yourself, so now it's time to let your ex be left alone for some duration in order to move on.

In short, leaving with integrity involves working diligently to be the bigger person. After all, you are the one who wanted to go and set everything into motion. If you find yourself having left a relationship without someone else in the wings, then you certainly should pat yourself on the back and be commended. You have left with integrity.

CHAPTER 24

BEGINNING TO DATE AFTER
THE BIG BREAKUP

I was always one of those people so hurt by the ending of a relationship, as I never did the leaving when I should have, that I was not interested in dating again for long periods of time. It was not uncommon for me to have a full year or more in between relationships. Unfortunately, I seemed to put all my attention on what was wrong with you that you couldn't do the relationship. My emotions were pulled furiously into the victim mode, certainly not by any rational choice, and there I would stay for long periods of time. However, viewing things through the perspective of a victim is in no way compatible with increasing self-realization. It keeps us from learning the lessons at hand and getting better results in future endeavors. This is what I learned…..

So you have arrived at this point again in your life. Some are excited at the idea and others cringe at the thought of getting out there again after such an emotional upheaval. You have hopefully reached a spot where you're okay being alone, but the idea of having someone special sounds nice. This calm, rational place is the indication that you are perhaps ready. All relationships have something to teach us- it's not really just about painful endings. Take the time to sit down and get clear on a few things before you venture out there again. Be sure that you can identify recognize your patterns, identify your "wants & needs" and act as your authentic self with the confidence to say what is on your mind from the word go.

Recognizing your patterns is perhaps one of the most important items you need to address. Look back at your previous relationships and identify the commonalities in the people you have chosen to gravitate towards. Do you choose partners who can't commit, partners who are controlling or partners with drug or alcohol dependence? Write these patterns down on a piece of paper to assess if you are again falling into these old habits in your new dating experiences. If you are, you need to address it immediately. In reality our patterns say something about us and not about our dumb luck in choosing partners. You have to take the time to figure out why you are drawn to these people in the first place.

Your second task is to identify your wants and needs. Get a piece of paper out and list these things. Needs are the non-negotiable items you simply must have, knowing yourself and who you are. Our needs have a lot to do with our value systems, as any solid relationship must have a fair degree of similarity in core values between the partners. If you are about honesty and integrity, you can't make yourself be okay with someone who is always trying to screw someone else over or never seems to be telling the whole truth. Wants are more like the icing on the cake. After you list these items take a harder look at them again. Many people often put these components in the wrong columns. You don't need someone who likes camping- you want someone who likes to camp. Remember, relationships are about sharing new experiences with each other, and your partner may not yet know that they like to camp. As you begin to date, ask yourself if the person you are interested in can truly meet your needs and optimally some of your wants.

Lastly, I can't say enough about being your authentic self from the very beginning. Too many people put forth a somewhat dishonest portrayal of who they are. This is not to say that they make things up. Rather, this incomplete portrait has more to do with not speaking up regarding your thoughts and feelings. If the person you are dating says or does something that bothers you, speak up and get clarification. The fear that they may go away if you do might just be a favor you need to take them up on.

It's okay to be you. Real love comes from a feeling of acceptance. You can't truly feel accepted if you aren't comfortable being yourself.

In short, you want to learn from past relationships. If you think that it has always been the other person that has caused the problems, you are probably not being honest with yourself. You have to assess what you could have done better in terms of communication, reactions and the like. You must approach each relationship in a different manor if you want different results. Contrary to popular belief, you have to work at having a good, fulfilling relationship just as you have to work at anything you want to be successful in life. This work is often about learning from past experience and changing the way you engage in love.

CHAPTER 25

DATING STAGES

I have always yearned for a successful, committed relationship from an early time in my life. I naively assumed that everyone felt the same way that I did. So, I was always crushed and hurt when relationships ended because for some reason I didn't think they would. I was not aware that a person could feel differently about having a relationship at different points in his or her life. This is what I learned…..

When it comes to dating, it is important to think about it in the context of various stages in order to have less disappointment and a better rate of success. Disappointment often ensues when two people meet and have very different ideas about what they are looking for at this particular point in their life. The three main stages one could be in when thinking about relationships include single, just dating and committed. It is important to identify what stage you are in, gain an understanding of the problems associated with people meeting at different stages and be willing to do the work necessary to propel yourself from one stage to the next.

Identifying what stage you are in is a necessary first step. Are you single and deep down desiring a committed relationship? This scenario is common for many people. However, in order to reach that final stage, you first have to be willing to go out there and swim around a while in the just dating stage. Plenty of people don't really like the just dating stage and all of the sorting, sifting and screening skills that are required to connect with someone with whom you are compatible. On the other hand, are you really in the just dating stage and having difficulty because you keep meeting people ready for a serious commitment? We are all operating at different stages at different times and it is primarily dictated by the events of a person's life.

Relationships are constantly beginning and constantly ending for everyone. The thoughts we form about that will affect everyone differently. For instance, someone who just went through a painful divorce may be an avowed single, while others are eager to jump right back into the just dating stage. Likewise, some people join Internet dating services for the sole purpose of just dating, yet others are in a serious search for a committed relationship. Some of the well-known dating services query for this very thing, so in theory we will know what stage a person is in and can make an appropriate choice. However, what someone says, regarding what they are looking for, and where they really are can often be incongruent. If however, you have decided to get serious about your search for love, you need to put some energy into it and get back out there.

Being willing to put yourself out in the world is the first step. Many venues exist to help people meet for relationships. Internet services are good, as they give you the opportunity to brush up on your sorting, sifting and screening skills. If you view it for just that, then you can avoid disappointment if you don't instantly make a love connection. Joining clubs, groups, volunteering and just participating in life will afford the opportunity to meet like-minded individuals for potential dating partners as well. You almost automatically ensure that you will at least have one factor in common from the start. If you are single and wishing for a committed relationship, you need to be sure you are out in the world and participating. You never know who you will meet and what you will find.

CHAPTER 26

THE EASE OF COMPATIBILITY

After a 10 year relationship ended and I lost the house, the dog and my precious plants, I realized that we had had virtually nothing in common. More importantly, we spoke different languages (figuratively speaking) and our core values were at odds. Too often I chased the idea of being in love, happy to be chosen and thankful again for unconsciously avoiding rejection. My criteria were clearly lacking in scope and size and therefore, I often ended up in relationships with individuals with whom I would never gravitate to for friendship. This is what I learned…..

Have you ever heard someone say, "It's not supposed to take that much work?" Have you ever heard the old cliché, "you'll know when it's right?"

There is a reason people make statements like that when referring to relationships. It's because they are true. Anyone who has achieved a strong, solid relationship knows this assertion to be fundamentally accurate. For those individuals who are still searching for a great relationship it may be something we understand only in theory, but it is crucial that we keep these ideas in the forefront of our minds when sorting and sifting through the dating process. Compatibility makes for a much smoother, easy union and operates on a variety of levels. As you continue your relationship quest, keep in mind the importance of compatibility in the realms of energy levels, core values and affection.

In my early years I never really understood, nor thought much about, how important it is to have some degree of compatibility in the level of energy of both individuals. I often hooked up with partners who told me I could never sit still or with whom I felt stifled because they never seemed to want to venture out in the world and be spontaneous together. We were definitely not compatible in energy levels. Through my eyes they were too sedate and through their eyes I was far too hyper. When I finally met up with a partner who had the same level of energy, all of the old complaints dissipated and a great deal of harmony existed in the air. Perhaps that harmony had a lot to do with the feeling of it "just being right." A lovely calm exists between two people with compatibility in energy levels, even if they are both high. In addition to energy levels, having similar core values is perhaps one of the most important areas in which two people must be compatible.

As I have said many times before congruity in core values is essential. If you value honesty, integrity and treating others with kindness, you can never truly be happy with someone who acts in a way that opposes those values. Yes, compromise is the cornerstone to any good relationship. Compromises have to be worked out when two individuals are different regarding traits such as cleaning, money and time. However, you will never be happy if you find yourself compromising on your core values. Relationships that are not compatible in this area have continual upheaval if both people are really being honest and fully speaking up about their true feelings. You should not be expected to compromise on your fundamental values, so keep this lesson in mind as you navigate the dating arena. As with core values, it is also important to have a degree of compatibility in the levels of affection you require.

I can't even begin to tell you the difficulties I see in my practice when two people are vastly different in the levels of affection they demonstrate towards each other. For many people, affection is a necessity just as breathing is to life. I would definitely be one of those people. Different reasons contribute to why someone not being highly affectionate. However, the answer to why does not change the fact that plenty of people will readily admit that they are not that affectionate.

Once again, this trait is not a right or wrong issue. It is merely one of compatibility. A lack of compatibility in this area almost inevitably leads to problems with sex as well. Two people who are not that affectionate will not be upset with each other if there isn't a lot of affection. You will save a lot of hurt feelings and upset if you are joined with someone who is more like you in this arena. It is the compatibility factor in this realm, and others, that helps make for a smooth relationship.

In short, compatibility makes relationship dynamics whole lot smoother. It is your job to assess the compatibility factor in the realms of energy levels, core values and affection. Compatibility then can be viewed as a "need" in a relationship just as any other type of need you will have. It is your job to insist that your needs be met, or move on to someone who can meet them. People are basically who they are until they choose to make changes for their own personal betterment. Therefore, they have to be acceptable as they are from the start. You cannot expect them to change. Look for compatibility and you will have a much smoother, happier relationship for the duration.

CHAPTER 27

LEARNING TO LOVE
WITHOUT EXPECTATION

It had never dawned on me that I had been giving so much just to get. I was always heading towards a project or rescue job, as it was here that I obviously had my greatest confidence in my ability to succeed. Over time, the criteria changed and I did scrutinize more and more with each successful relationship. I drew the line at drinking problems and unemployment, but I still found myself gravitating to those people who needed emotional rescuing. I'm a caretaker by nature and probably always will be. However, I finally decided to find my voice, begin to speak up and state my boundaries. I in essence treated myself with love and it began to be returned. This is what I learned.......

Have you ever heard yourself saying, "Why doesn't the one I love ever love me back?" Well, maybe you are loved back, but just not in the way you want it to look. Maybe you are loved by many people but are not taking the time to appreciate it because your expectations are not being met. Helping others needs to come from the heart, not from a sense of giving to get. Are you truly giving to others from the heart, or is there something you are seeking always lurking in the recesses of your mind? Do you excessively jump in at the start of a relationship and start a pattern of doing too much? It is an important question that we must ask ourselves. People may excessively give for a number of reasons. Common catalysts include thinking that you need to give in order to be valued by your partner, gravitating to individuals that need "rescuing" or continuing a pattern you have always participated in which has become unhealthy and needs to be changed.

Feeling loved and valued by another is a beautiful. However, you ultimately want someone to feel this for you because of who you are, not for the good deeds that you do. Perhaps this behavior of excess giving was modeled to you by one of your parents. Or, perhaps this conduct comes from having lower self-esteem. It can sometimes feel as if you need to give at a high level or you will not be loved back. The danger in this act is that it starts an uneven pattern or dynamic in the relationship from the very onset. And, the recipient of the excessive giving may begin to feel as if they will never be able to love you as much as you love them. This unevenness in give and take can then begin to feel like way too much pressure in the relationship. Any aspect of a relationship that is out of balance almost always becomes problematic down the road. And if you give inordinately, you invariably set yourself up for feeling taken for granted and unappreciated. Excessively giving or doing for another is not in balance. Take the time to ask yourself if dynamic is occurring in your relationship and begin to address it now. Identify the ways in which you may be out of balance with your giving and make a conscious effort to pull back in these areas.

Rescuing another is also something that also drives giving to get and keeps us from learning to love without expectation. Many clients come into my office and identify a pattern of rescuing in their relationships. What are some of the reasons that one may be prone to seeking out people to rescue in their romantic lives? By its very nature, rescuing often results in accolades of gratitude coming to you by the recipient of your efforts. This adoration feels good, especially for the person looking to others to make them feel loved. And once we get this feeling, we want more and more. Rescuing also puts you in the take-charge mode and this position may be the only role in a relationship in which you are comfortable. If you have a habit of excessively giving, picking someone to be rescued lends itself perfectly to this pattern. However, this set-up will again lead to starting the relationship out on an uneven footing and can cause problems later. If you are rescuing someone who doesn't have his or her life together you may likewise be setting up a parent/child type of relationship right from the beginning. Eventually, the rescued person may grow up and the efforts once appreciated will start to become resented. Rescuing also takes your energy away from you and allows it to become solely focused on another, which is never good for a well-rounded existence in life.

If this behavior of uneven giving is all that you have ever experienced in your relationships, it is time to actively start doing something to correct the imbalance. This pattern is unhealthy and has probably never gotten you the result you want. Stop giving so much and stop rescuing. What makes a person truly feel good in a relationship is some degree of reciprocation from their partner. Excessive giving leaves no room for reciprocity to occur and rescuing puts a wrench into obtaining this occurrence from the very beginning. Learning to love without expectation is something that we should all aspire to in the process of life and personal growth. Learning to love without expectation allows us to stop the pattern of giving to get, as we are giving from the heart and not hoping for something in return. The need to play out a pattern of overly giving is what guides us to the wrong potential partners in the first place. Give to others at a balanced pace and allow the love to be returned. Even if they don't love you back in the way you had hoped, give them the opportunity to love you back in the way they can.

CPSIA information can be obtained at www.ICGtesting.com
Printed in the USA
LVOW082341090112

263117LV00001B/1/P